THIS BOOK BELONGS TO

Foods that are full of color,

from yellow to green,

provide fuel for our bodies

like a machine.

There are so many foods

that we can discover,

so let's explore

and eat more colors!

Almonds

With an oval shape and tan color
it's flavor is quite delicious.
Almonds contain healthy fats
and help our body fight sickness.
A seed that's good for your heart
and great to share with a buddy,
containing minerals that help keep you alert
so you can focus at school and study.

Apples

Either red, green, or yellow,

when this sweet fruit is picked,

apples boost our immune system

and keep us from getting sick.

Great for our hearts,

so go ahead, take another bite!

They're great for cleaning teeth,

so you can show off those pearly whites.

Asparagus

Loaded with nutrients

and grown when spring time is near.

This weapon fights disease,

that's why it's shaped like a spear.

Asparagus can make you happier

sending nutrients to your brain

helping your body heal itself

even bone strength is maintained.

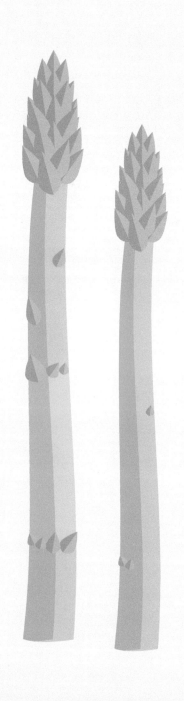

Avocado

Named the alligator pear.

It has one large seed

with different colors,

from black to green.

A lot of vitamins

this berry includes.

This makes the avocado

a super food!

Banana

Wearing a yellow jacket
and grown in warm weather.
When you have a tummy ache
this may make it feel better.
Giving our body energy
and not only for monkeys,
bananas are good for our muscles
and their taste is very yummy.

Beans

Black beans, pinto beans,
lima beans, and kidney.
These are only a few beans,
there are so many.
They make you feel full
with plenty of healthy benefits.
They're good for your belly.
Add them to any dish.

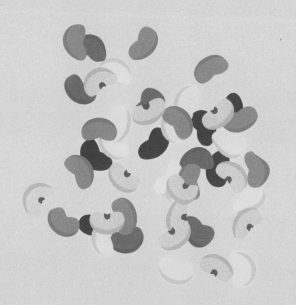

Blueberry

Small in size

even when they are grown.

You may be surprised,

this fruit is good for your bones.

A sweet snack,

blueberry is it's name

they keep your heart healthy

and are good for your brain.

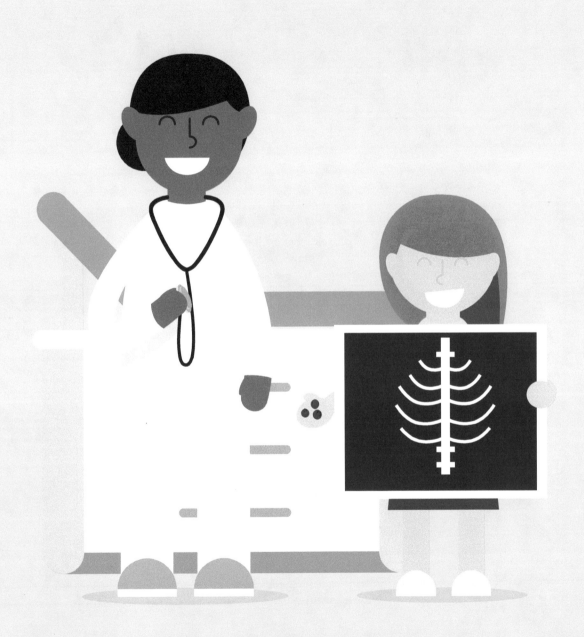

Broccoli

The top of this plant
has tiny green leaves,
making them look
like very small trees.
Lots of minerals
this vegetable brings.
Cleaning your body,
removing bad things.

Carrot

Grown underground
you may find it funny,
that this orange vegetable
isn't only for bunnies.
Carrots help improve eyesight
and clean your teeth.
This makes the carrot
an awesome vegetable to eat.

Celery

A crispy stalk

containing lots of water.

This crunchy green snack,

taste great with peanut butter.

It helps calm nerves

and even lowers blood pressure.

Strengthens bones

and helps with food digestion.

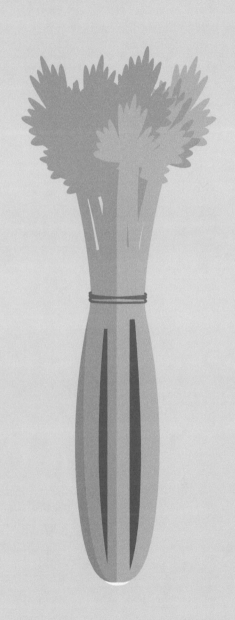

Grapes

Grapes are delicious finger foods
that are quite amazing.
There are so many different uses for them.
When dried, we call them raisins.
Grapes help prevent cavities
improving your dental health,
and are also good for your brain
by improving your mental health.

Guava

Shaped like an apple
and green like an iguana,
a tropical super fruit
better known as guava.
With so many health benefits
where do we begin?
It's great for eyesight, upset stomach,
brain health and skin.

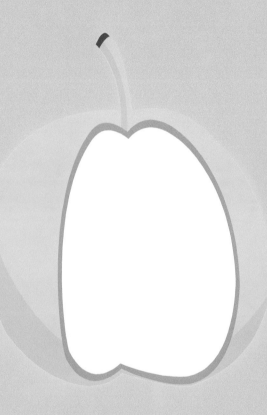

Kale

Very high in minerals

with leaves that are green or purple.

Related to the cabbage

and one of the healthiest foods, for certain.

When it comes to complete health,

kale definitely does it's duty.

It taste great with other fruits,

try blending it in a smoothie.

Pineapple

Resembling a large pinecone
with an outer shell that's spiny.
A tropical fruit that's packed with juice,
and flavor is far from tiny.
Eating pineapples can help reduce swelling
whenever you have a bruise.
They're filled with lots of vitamin C
used to fight coughs, colds, and flu.

Raspberry

Plump juicy berries

that are refreshingly sweet.

Excellent for heart health,

and satisfying to eat.

Small and brightly colored

you could call it nature's candy.

If you need to improve your memory,

raspberries can come in handy.

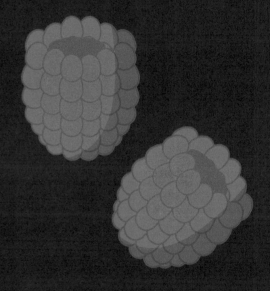

Spinach

When it comes to energy,

there aren't many that can compare.

These dark leafy greens

are important for skin and hair.

Great for growing bodies,

you can't go wrong.

Always eat your spinach,

it will make you big and strong.

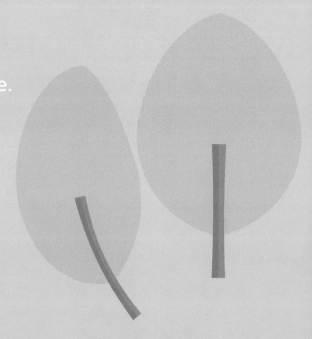

Strawberry

Its taste is very sweet

and red color, a work of art.

Not really a fruit or a berry,

but shaped like a heart.

A member of the rose family

having seeds on the outside.

With high amounts of nutrients,

strawberries are definitely worth a try.

Sweet Potatoes

Cook them roasted,

or cook them steamed,

or eat them grilled

with leafy greens.

Looking for a potato that's sweet?

This will do the trick.

Add sweet potatoes to any meal

to help keep from getting sick.

Turnip

Turnips are a root vegetable
favoring a large radish.
With dark-green leafy tops,
usually eaten as a side dish.
Supplying your bones and teeth
with nutrients that keep them mighty.
Fighting against many illnesses
keeping the inside of your body tidy.

Watermelon

It may seem obvious,
that given this fruit's name
it's filled with water
but its taste is far from plain.
A thirst-quenching treat
that's a little bit crunchy.
If you need a boost of energy,
try watermelon when you're hungry.

Watermelon
For Sale!

Foods that are colorful,

foods that are bright

will help us all live

a healthier life.

We only have one body

and won't get another.

So let's take care of the one we have

and eat more colors!

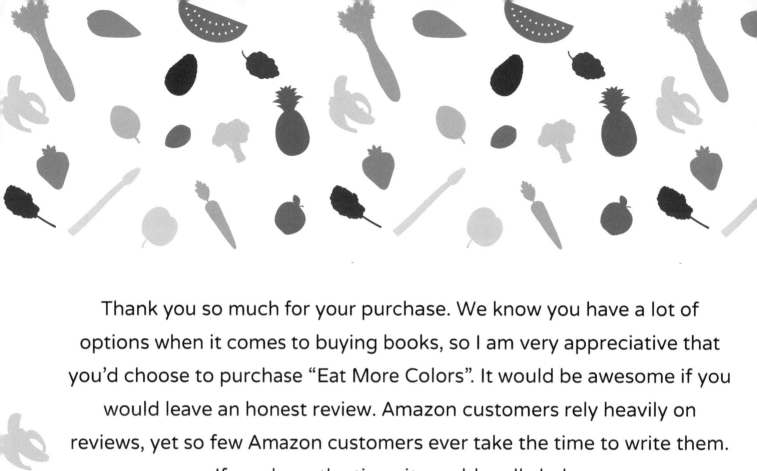

Thank you so much for your purchase. We know you have a lot of options when it comes to buying books, so I am very appreciative that you'd choose to purchase "Eat More Colors". It would be awesome if you would leave an honest review. Amazon customers rely heavily on reviews, yet so few Amazon customers ever take the time to write them. If you have the time, it would really help.

www.eatmorecolors.com

Printed in the USA
CPSIA information can be obtained
at www.ICGtesting.com
LVHW061114201123
764256LV00002BA/2

9 781987 639056